# The
# World's Best
# Dirty
# Limericks

# The World's Best Dirty Limericks

Introduction by Harold H. Hart

ANGUS
& ROBERTSON
PUBLISHERS

*ANGUS & ROBERTSON PUBLISHERS*

*Unit 4, Eden Park, 31 Waterloo Road,*
*North Ryde, NSW, Australia 2113, and*
*16 Golden Square, London W1R 4BN,*
*United Kingdom*

*First published by*
*Hart Publishing Co., Inc., USA, in 1970*
*First published in Australia by*
*Angus & Robertson Publishers in 1982*
*First published in the United Kingdom by*
*Angus & Robertson UK in 1985*
*Reprinted 1984, 1986 (twice)*

*ISBN 0 207 14650 0*

*Printed in Great Britain by*
*Hazell Watson & Viney Limited*

# Introduction

The limerick packs laughs anatomical
Into space that is quite economical.
    But the good ones I've seen
    So seldom are clean —
And the clean ones so seldom are comical.


The limerick's an art form complex
Whose contents run chiefly to sex;
    It's famous for virgins
    And masculine urgin's,
And vulgar erotic effects.


The limerick, peculiar to English,
Is a verse form that's hard to extinguish.
    Once Congress in session
    Decreed its suppression
But people got around it by writing the
   last line without any rhyme or meter.


God's plan made a hopeful beginning
But man spoiled his chances by sinning.
    We trust that the story
    Will end in God's glory —
But at present the other side's winning.

The limerick is now an abiding part of our literature. A highly disciplined verse form, compact and clever, it tells a story in only five lines. Unlike most basic forms of English verse, such as the sonnet and the triolet, the limerick was not borrowed from other countries but is indigenously English, perhaps the only form in poetry that can be claimed to be an original English creation.

Undoubtedly, the limerick is the most quoted of all verse forms extant today. From the drawing room to the classroom, whether recited in a surreptitious whisper or blared forth uproariously, the limerick has captivated almost every echelon of society. Popular everywhere, it has especially become the darling of the intellectual.

The limerick reflects the temper of its day. Additions to this great fund of versification have been made by outstanding poets and publicists. Some of the most widely recited limericks have been ascribed, perhaps aprocryphally, to Alfred Lord Tennyson, Norman Douglas, Eugene Field, Don Marquis, Heywood Broun, Woodrow Wilson, among others.

Back in the 1860s, Edward Lear penned these rhythmical five-line ditties for children. But the form soon bounded out of the nursery onto the campus; and from there into the market place, the counting house, and the army. Once out on the streets and in full contact with the foibles, frustrations, and fantasies of the common folk, the limerick began to reflect the thoughts of the people more and more plain-spokenly. The more pungent, punchy, and bawdy, the more easily were these verses remembered, and the more frequently were they quoted.

In the preface to his delicious book *Some Limericks*, Norman Douglas acknowledges that the verses in his collection might be considered obscene. "Why, so they are;" he wrote, "and whoever suffers from that trying form of degeneration, which is horrified at coarseness, had better close this book at once."

What is considered coarse and not coarse is largely a cultural matter, and such judgments change in every age. I remember when I was a boy it was considered quite tasteless to refer to a woman as pregnant. Polite society proscribed all reference as to how the two billion people who were then on the earth happened to get there. The most that any well-mannered person was permitted to delicately say was that a woman was "in a family way." In that day, no one was supposed to mention bodily functions. Euphemisms camouflaged all trips to the bathroom. During the same era, a woman who showed as much as a naked knee at a bathing resort was considered lewd.

Today, the era of the bikini witnesses a drastically altered level of acceptable idiom. Though bluenoses may deplore, there is hardly anything that is considered sacrosanct and unmentionable. With the liberalization of our mores, it is now appropriate to publish some immortal verses which, heretofore, were reserved for stag parties.

The editor of this volume has long been an enthusiast and collector of the limerick. In this book he presents verses which have particularly tickled his fancy. Many of these poems are bawdy; some are devilishly clever; all, it is hoped, will amuse.

The subjects treated by the anonymous authors of these stanzas run the entire gamut of sexual activity. Fantasy has no limits, and many verses rise to heights of superlative exaggeration.

Some of the limericks in this book are printed here for the very first time. They are the creations of old friends and forgotten acquaintances of a past day, and I would only be able to make a guess as to who wrote what. No credits appear in these pages for any of these limericks, old or "new," because in no instance is the authorship really ascertainable. If any person has been slighted by such omission, this has not been done deliberately and forgiveness is begged. In any case, the unknown author may derive the private satisfaction of knowing his creation may now become immortalized.

# The
# World's Best
# Dirty
# Limericks

There was a young lady in Reno

Who lost all her dough playing keeno.

But she lay on her back

And opened her crack—

And now she owns the casino.

There was a young girl in Berlin

Who was raped by an elderly Finn.

Though he diddled his best

And screwed her with zest,

She kept asking, "Hey, Pop! Is it in?"


A big Catholic layman named Fox

Makes his living by sucking off cocks.

In spells of depression

He goes to confession,

And jacks off the priest in his box.

A lady while dining at Crewe

Found an elephant's whang in her stew.

Said the waiter, "Don't shout,

Or wave it about,

Or the rest will be wanting one, too."

There was a young man from Montmartre

Who was famed far and wide for his fart.

When they said, "What a noise!"

He replied with great poise,

"When I fart, sir, I fart from the heart."



There was a young farmer of Nant,

Whose conduct was both gay and gallant;

For he fucked all his dozens

Of nieces and cousins,

In addition, of course, to his aunt.

There was a young fellow from Florida

Who liked a friend's wife, so he borrowed her.

 When they got into bed

 He cried, "God strike me dead!

Now this ain't a cunt—it's a corridor!"




There was a young fellow named Kimble

Whose prick was exceedingly nimble

 But so fragile, so slender

 So dainty and tender

He kept it encased in a thimble.

A cheerful young golfer named Kroch

Gave his tee shot a hundred-yard sock.

It doesn't sound far

For the man who shoots par,

But 'twas done with the end of his cock.


There was a young girl of Llewellyn

Whose breasts were as big as a melon.

They were big, it is true,

But her cunt was big too,

Like a bifocal, full-color, aerial view of

Cape Horn and the Straits of Magellan.

There was a smart miss had a hernia

Who said to her doctor, "Goldernia,

 When improving my middle

 Be sure you don't fiddle

With matters that do not concernia."

A flatulent nun of Hawaii

One Easter eve supped on papaya;

 Then honored the Passover

 By turning her ass over

And obliging with Handel's *Messiah.*

There was a young man of Cawnpore

Whose tool was so awfully sore

From slapping and rubbing,

And pulling and drubbing,

It was useless for what it was for.


There was a young lady of Rheims,

Who amazingly pissed in four streams.

A friend poked around

And a coat button found

Wedged tightly in one of her seams.

There was an old lady of Cheadle

Who sat down in church on a needle.

The needle, though blunt,

Penetrated her cunt,

But was promptly removed by the beadle.

A farmer I know named O'Doole

Has a long and incredible tool.

He can use it to plow,

Or to diddle a cow,

Or just as a cue-stick at pool.

There was a young student named Jones

Who'd reduce any maiden to moans

By his wonderful knowledge,

Acquired in college,

Of nineteen erogenous zones.




There was a young Turkish cadet—

And this is the damnedest one yet—

His tool was so long

And incredibly strong

He could bugger six Greeks *en brochette*.

There once was a gangster named Brown,

The wiliest bastard in town.

He was caught by the G-men

Shooting his semen

Where the cops would all slip and fall down.



A mortician who practiced in Fife

Made love to the corpse of his wife.

"How would I know, Judge?

She was cold, did not budge—

Just the same as she'd acted in life."

There was a young person of Goring,

Who made a small hole in the flooring.

He lined it all round

Then laid on the ground,

—Declared it was cheaper than whoring.


There was a young man from Toledo

Who was cursed with excessive libido.

To fuck, to screw,

And to fornicate, too,

Were the three major points of his credo.

There was an old party of Lyme

Who married three wives at one time;

When asked, "Why the third?"

He replied, "One's absurd,

And bigamy, Sir, is a crime."




There was a young fellow named Sweeney

Whose girl was a terrible meanie.

The hatch of her snatch

Had a catch that would latch—

She could only be screwed by Houdini.

$A$ bather whose clothing was strewed

By breezes that left her quite nude

    Saw a man come along,

    And, unless I am wrong,

You expected this line to be lewd.

A prissy old maid named Miss Hannah
Wrote Burbank a note in this manner:
Could you spare a few hours
From your shrubs and your flowers
And put a pulse in the banana?

There was a young man of Japan
Whose limericks never would scan.
When someone asked why,
He would slowly reply,
"Perhaps it's because I always try to get
as many dirty words in the last
line as I possibly can."

That naughty old Sappho of Greece

Said, "What I prefer to a piece

   Is to have my pudenda

   Rubbed hard by the enda

The little pink nose of my niece."


I once knew a very queer lass

Who had a triangular ass.

   Now it might sound absurd

   But the shape of her turd

Was a stately pyramidal mass!

There was a young man of high station

Who was found by a pious relation

    Making love in a ditch

    To—I won't say a bitch—

But a lady of no reputation.

A thrifty old man named McEwen

Inquired, "Why bother with screwing?

    It's safer and cleaner

    To finger your wiener,

And besides you can see what you're doing."

T here was a young harlot from Kew

Who filled her vagina with glue.

    She said with a grin,

    "If they pay to get in,

They'll pay to get out of it, too."

There was a young lady from Brent

Whose old man's pecker got bent,

She said with a sigh,

"Oh, why must it die?

Let's fill it with Portland Cement."


There once was a Bishop of Treet

Who decided to be indiscreet,

But after one round

To his horror he found

You repeat, and repeat, and repeat!

Moaned Tessie, the whore, "In this land,

I've met bastards who thought it was grand

To retire, when inclined,

With sex problems in mind,

And awake with solution in hand."

There was a young girl from France

Who jumped on a bus in a trance.

Six passengers fucked her,

Besides the conductor,

And the driver shot twice in his pants.

A pansy by name of Ben Bloom

Took a lesbian up to his room,

They talked the whole night

As to who had the right

To do what, with which, and to whom.

There was a young sailor named Bates

Who danced the fandango on skates.

But a fall on his cutlass

Has rendered him nutless,

And practically useless on dates.



A freshman with visions Elysian

Once screwed an appendix incision,

But the girl of his choice

Could hardly rejoice

At this horrible lack of precision.

There was a young tar from the sea

Who screwed a baboon in a tree;

The result was most horrid,

All ass and no forehead,

Four balls and a purple goatee.


A pretty young harlot of Crete

Used to hawk her meat in the street.

Ambling out one fine day

In a most casual way,

She clapped up the whole British fleet.

There was a young maid from Madras

Who had a magnificent ass;

　　Not rounded and pink,

　　As you probably think —

It was grey, had long ears, and ate grass.

A young lad with passions gingery

Tore a hole in his sister's best lingerie.

He pinched her behind,

And made up his mind

To add incest to insult and injury.

There was a young lawyer named Rex

Who was sadly deficient in sex.

Arraigned for exposure

He said with composure,

*"De minimis non curat lex."** *

---

*The law is not concerned with trifles.

There was a young woman of Florence,

Who was looked on with general abhorrence

    In an amorous crush

    Her bladder would flush,

And the stuff came out in great torrents.



There was a young Catholic named Alice,

Who peed in the Bishop's new chalice;

    But that worthy agreed

    That 'twas done out of need,

And not out of Protestant malice.

There was a lewd nude from Bermuda

Who was shrewd, but I proved to be shrewder.

    She said, "It is lewd

      To be screwed in the nude."

But I grew lewder, & shrewder, & screwed her.

There was a young fellow from France

Who waited ten years for his chance.

    Then he muffed it.

An Argentine gaucho named Bruno

Once said, "There is one thing I do know:

A woman is fine

And a sheep is divine—

But a llama's Numero Uno!"

"Austerity now is the fashion,"

Remarked a young lady with passion.

Then she glanced at the bed,

And quietly said,

"There's one thing no nation can ration."


A charming young lady from Brussels

Takes pride in her vaginal muscles.

For any erection

Her timing's perfection

And she never hurries—she hustles.

There was a young plumber named Lee,

Who plumbed his girl down by the sea;

    Said the lady, "Stop plumbing!

    I hear someone coming."

Said the plumber, still plumbing, "That's me."


An impish young fellow named James

Had a passion for idiot games.

    He lighted the hair

    Of his lady's affair

And laughed as she peed through the flames.

Said a printer pretending to wit:
"There are certain bad words we omit.
   It would sully our art
   To print the word f - - - ,
And we never, oh never, say sh - - !"




A forward young fellow named Tarr
Had a habit of goosing his Ma;
   "Go pester your sister,"
   She said when he kissed her,
"I've trouble enough with your Pa."

There was a young lady named Banker,

Who slept while her ship lay at anchor.

She awoke in dismay

When she heard the mate say:

"Hi! Hoist up the top-sheet and spanker!"

There was a young lady of Ealing,

Endowed with such delicate feeling,

When she read on the door:

"Don't piss on the floor"—

She lay down and pissed on the ceiling.

These words spoke the king of Siam,

"For women I don't care a damn,

But a fat-bottomed boy

Is my pride and my joy.

You may call me a bugger. I am!"

There was a young lady of Chichester

Who made all the saints in their niches stir.

One morning, at matins,

Her breasts in white satins

Made the Bishop of Chichester's britches stir.

There was a young fellow named Bliss

Whose sex life was strangely amiss,

For even with Venus

His recalcitrant penis

Would seldom do better than t
h
i
s.

There was a young lady of Dexter

Whose husband exceedingly vexed her,

    For whenever they'd start

    He'd unfailingly fart

With a blast that damn nearly unsexed her.


There's an over-sexed lady named Whyte

Who insists on a dozen a night.

    A fellow named Cheddar

    Had the brashness to wed her—

And his chance of survival is slight.

Nymphomaniacal Alice

Used a dynamite stick for a phallus;

    They found her vagina

    In North Carolina

And half of her ass-hole in Dallas.


A dentist, young Doctor Malone,

Got a charming girl patient alone;

    And, in his depravity,

    He filled the wrong cavity—

And my how his practice has grown!

There was a young fellow from Boston

Who rode around in an Austin.

There was room for his ass

And a gallon of gas,

But his balls hung outside, and he lost 'em.

There was a young lady of Twickenham

Who used to take cocks without pickin' 'em.

    She'd kneel on the sod,

    And pray to her God

To lengthen & strengthen & thicken 'em.




There was a young man from Australia

Who painted his ass like a dahlia.

    The colors were fine;

    The drawing—divine!

But the smell was a terrible failure!

There was a young man of Khartoum

Who lured a poor girl to her doom.

He not only fucked her,

And buggered and sucked her—

But left her to pay for the room.


Three lovely young girls from St. Thomas

Attended dance-halls in pajamas.

They were fondled all summer

By sax, bass, and drummer—

I'm surprised that by now they're not mamas.

A lecherous Bishop of Peoria,

In a state of constant euphoria,

Enjoyed having fun

With a whore or a nun

While chanting the *Sanctus* and *Gloria.*

E vangeline Alice Du Bois

Committed a dreadful faux pas.

She loosened a stay

In her décolleté,

Exposing her je ne sais quoi.

A man with venereal fear

Had intercourse in his wife's ear.

    She said, "I don't mind,

    Except that I find

When the telephone rings, I don't hear."

Said a man of his small Morris Minor

"For petting, it couldn't be finer;

But for love's consummation

A wagon called station

Would offer a playground diviner."

A timorous maiden named Harriet

Dreamt she was raped in a chariot—

By seventeen sailors,

Four monks, and two tailors

Mohammed and Judas Iscariot!

There was a young fellow named Hill

Who took a uranium pill;

    His entrails corroded,

    His belly exploded,

And his balls were found in Brazil.




A remarkable race are the Persians,

They have such peculiar diversions;

    They make love all the day

    In the regular way,

And all night—they practice perversions.

A rascal far gone in lechery

Lured maids to their doom by his treachery.

He invited them in

For the purpose of sin,

Though he said 'twas to look at his etchery.



A crooner who lived in West Shore

Caught both of his balls in a door.

Now his mezzo-soprano

Is rather piano

Though he was a loud basso before.

Said the mythical King of Algiers

To his harem assembled, "My dears,

You may think it odd of me

But I'm tired of sodomy;

Tonight's for you ladies" (*Loud cheers!*)

There was a young fellow named Skinner

Who took a young lady to dinner.

    They started to dine

    At a quarter past nine—

And at twenty to ten it was in 'er.

    The dinner? No, Skinner.

    Skinner was in 'er *before* dinner.


There was a young fellow named Tupper

Who took a young lady to supper.

    They sat down to dine,

    At a quarter to nine,

And at twenty to ten it was up 'er.

    Not the supper—not Tupper—it was

    some son-of-a-bitch named Skinner!

There was a young fellow named Fyfe

Whose marriage was ruined for life,

    For he had an aversion

    To every perversion

And only liked screwing his wife.

Well, one year the poor woman struck

And she wept, and she cursed at her luck,

    "Oh, where has it gotten us

    This goddamn monotonous

Fuck after fuck after fuck?"

There was an old maid of Duluth,

Who wept when she thought of her youth,

Remembering chances

She missed at school dances,

And once in a telephone booth.




There once was a girl named McGoffin

Who was diddled amazingly often.

At sex, never bested,

She never was rested

Until she was screwed in her coffin.

There was a young blade of Connaught
Whose prick was remarkably short.
When he got into bed
His lady friend said,
"This isn't a prick, it's a wart."


There was an old man of Tagore
Who tried out his cook on the floor;
He used Bridget's twidget
To fidget his digit,
And now she won't cook any more.

There was a young fellow named Wyatt

Who kept a big girl on the quiet;

    But down on the wharf

    He kept a dwarf,

In case he should go on a diet.

Well screwed was a boy named Delpasse

By all of the lads in his class.

He said, with a yawn,

"Now the novelty's gone

And it's only a pain in the ass."



There was a young monk of Dundee

Who complained that it hurt him to pee.

He said, "Pax vobiscum!

Now why won't the piss come?

I'm afraid I've the C-L-A-P."

There was an old Count of Swoboda

Who would not pay a whore what he owed her.

So with great *savoir-faire*

She stood on a chair,

And pissed in his whiskey-and-soda.




There was a young man named Hughes

Who swore off all kinds of booze.

He said, "When I'm muddled

My senses get fuddled,

And I pass up too many screws."

A habit obscene and unsavory

Holds the Bishop of Wessex in slavery.

With maniacal howls

He deflowers young owls

Which he keeps in an underground aviary.

There was a young girl of Penzance

Who decided to take just one chance.

So she let herself go

In the arms of her beau—

Now all of her sisters are aunts.

There was a young girl named Ann Heuser

Who swore that no man could surprise her.

But Pabst took a chance,

Found a Schlitz in her pants,

And now she is sadder Budweiser.


A whimsical fellow named Block

Could beat the bass drum with his cock.

With a special erection

He could play a selection

From Johann Sebastian Bach.

There once was a young man from Greenwich

Whose balls were all covered with spinach;

    So long was his tool

    It was wound on a spool

In-ich, by in-ich, by in-ich!


There was a young man from Berlin

Whose tool was the size of a pin.

    Said his girl with a laugh

    As she fondled that shaft,

"Well, *this* won't be much of a sin."

There was a lovely young miss

Who went down to the river to read.

A young man in a punt

Stuck an oar in her eye

And now she has to wear glasses!

Did you hear about young Henry Lockett?

He was blown down the street by a rocket.

The force of the blast

Blew his balls up his ass,

And his pecker was found in his pocket.

There was a young woman of Croft

Who played with herself in a loft,

Having reasoned that candles

Could never cause scandals,

Besides which they did not go soft.

There was a young man from Sioux Falls

Renowned in vaudeville halls;

His favorite trick

Was to stand on his prick

And then slide off the stage on his balls!

There was a young lady at sea

Who complained that it hurt her to pee.

"Aha!" said the mate,

"That accounts for the state

Of the cook and the captain and me."

There was a young lady of Wantage

Of whom the Town Clerk took advantage.

    Said the County Surveyor,

    "Of course you must pay her:

You've altered the line of her frontage."

There were two young ladies of Birmingham,

And this is the story concerning 'em:

    They lifted the frock

    And diddled the cock

Of the Bishop as he was confirming 'em.

The Bishop was nobody's fool—

He'd been to a large public school;

    He took down his britches

    And diddled those bitches

With his ten-inch Episcopal tool.

But that didn't bother those two;

They said as the Bishop withdrew:

    "Oh, the Vicar is quicker

    And thicker and slicker

And longer and stronger than you."

There was a young fellow from Sparta,

A really magnificent farter,

On the strength of one bean

He'd fart *God Save the Queen,*

And Beethoven's *Moonlight Sonata.*

He could vary, with proper persuasion,

His fart to suit any occasion.

He could fart like a flute,

Like a lark, like a lute,

This highly fartistic Caucasian.

He'd fart a gavotte for a starter,

And fizzle a fine serenata.

He could play on his anus

*The Coriolanus:*

Oof, boom, er-tum, tootle, hum tah-dah!

He was great in the *Christmas Cantata,*

He could double-stop fart *The Toccata,*

    He'd boom from his ass

    *Bach's B-Minor Mass,*

And in counterpoint, *La Traviata.*

Spurred on by a very high wager

With an envious German named Bager,

    He'd proceeded to fart

    The complete oboe part

Of the Haydn *Octet in B-major.*

The selection was tough, I admit,

But it did not dismay him one bit,

    Then, with ass thrown aloft

    He suddenly coughed...

And collapsed in a shower of shit.

"For the tenth time, dull Daphnis," said Chloe,

"You have told me my bosom is snowy;

  You have made much fine verse on

  Each part of my person,

Now *do* something—there's a good boy!"




There was a young German named Ringer

Entertaining an opera singer,

  Said he, with a grin,

  "Well, I've sure got it in!"

Said she, "You mean that ain't your finger?"

There was a young lady named White

Found herself in a terrible plight:

A mucker named Tucker

Had struck her, the fucker—

The bugger, the bastard, the shite!

A newlywed couple from Goshen

Spent their honeymoon sailing the ocean.

    In twenty-eight days

    They got laid eighty ways—

Imagine such fucking devotion!

There was a young man of Cape Horn

Who wished he had never been born;

    And he wouldn't have been

    If his father had seen

That the end of the rubber was torn.

Said a lassie on one of her larks,

"It's more fun indoors than in parks.

    You feel more at ease,

    Your ass doesn't freeze,

And strollers don't make snide remarks."

There was a young girl of Baroda

Who built an erotic pagoda;

    The walls of its halls

    Were festooned with the balls

And the tools of the fools who bestrode her.

On a maiden a man once begat

Bouncing triplets named Nat, Tat, and Pat;

'Twas fun in the breeding

But hell in the feeding:

She hadn't a spare tit for Tat.

The Reverend Mr Uprightly

Was cuckolded daily and nightly

He murmured, "Dear, dear!

I would fain interfere,

If I knew how to do it politely."

A fearless young spermatozoa

Remarked to an ovum, "Helloa!

    We'd make a fine foetus,

    But I fear she'd mistreat us —

Where I come from they say she's a whoah!"


A n old maid in the land of Aloha

Got wrapped in the coils of a Boa.

    And as the snake squeezed

    The old maid, not displeased,

Cried, "Darling! I love it! Samoa!"

While Titian was mixing rose-madder,

His model posed nude on a ladder.

Her position, to Titian,

Suggested coition,

So he climbed up the ladder and had 'er.


There was a young lady whose joys

Were achieved with incomparable poise.

She could have an orgasm

With scarcely a spasm —

She could fart without making a noise!

A weary old lecher named Blott

Took a luscious young blonde to his yacht.

Too lazy to rape her,

He made darts out of paper,

Which he leisurely tossed at her twat.

A young curate, just new to the cloth,

At sex was surely no sloth.

> He preached masturbation

> To his whole congregation,

And was washed down the aisle on the froth.

A Bishop whose see was Vermont

Used to jerk himself off in the font.

> The baptistry stank

> With an odor most rank,

And no one would sit up in front.

A young violinist in Rio

Was seducing a lady named Cleo.

As she took down her panties,

She said, "No *andantes;*

I want this *allegro con brio!*"


There was a young girl from Sofia

Who succumbed to her lover's desire.

She said, "It's a sin,

But now that it's in,

Could you shove it a few inches higher!"

There once was a harlot at Yale

With her price-list tatooed on her tail.

And on her behind

For the sake of the blind

She had it embroidered in Braille.


The Shah of the Empire of Persia

Lay for days in a sexual merger,

When the Queen asked the Shah

"Won't you ever withdraw?"

He replied with a yawn, "It's inertia."

There was a young lady of Norway

Who hung by her toes in a doorway.

She said to her beau:

"Just look at me, Joe,

I think I've discovered one more way."

There was a young fellow named Gluck

Who found himself shit out of luck.

Though he petted and wooed,

When he tried to get screwed

He found virgins don't give a fuck.




An old archeologist, Throstle,

Discovered a marvelous fossil.

He knew from its bend

And the knob on the end

'Twas the peter of Paul the Apostle.

A trucker by name of McBride

Had a young whore that he hired

To fuck while out trucking,

But trucking *plus* fucking

Got him so fucking tired he got fired.




There was a young man of Devizes

Whose balls were of two different sizes.

The one was so small

'Twas nothing at all—

But the other—it won several prizes!

There once was a Bruce from Newcastle

Who rolled up a turd in a parcel;

He sent it by plane

to a poofter in Spain,

To show him the size of his arse-hole.

There was a young lady of Worcester

Who complained that many men goosed her.

So over her caper

She laid some sandpaper

Now they goose her much less than  they used ter.


There once was a lady from Arden

Who sucked off a man in a garden.

He said, "My dear Flo,

Where does all that stuff go?"

And she said, "*(swallow hard)*—I beg pardon?"

There was a young lady from Tottenham

Whose manners—well, she'd forgotten 'em.

While at tea at the vicar's,

She kicked off her knickers,

Explaining she felt much too hot in 'em.


There was a young man of Kildare

Who was fucking a girl on the stair.

The bannister broke,

But he doubled his stroke

And finished her off in mid-air.

There was a young couple named Kelly

Who were forced to walk belly to belly

Because in their haste

They used library paste

For what they thought was vaginal jelly.

There was a young fellow named Bart

Who strained every shit through a fart.

Each tip-tapered turd

Was the very last word

In this deft and most intricate art.

A flatulent Roman named Titus

Was taken with sudden colitis;

And the venerable Forum

Lost most of its quorum

As he farted up half of the situs.

There was a young lady from Spain

Whose face was exceedingly plain,

But her cunt had a pucker

That made the men fuck her,

Again, and again, and again.


A pathetic old maid of Bordeaux

Fell in love with a dashing young beau.

To arrest his regard

She would squat in his yard

And appealingly piss in the snow.

Sobbed the wife of a worrisome veep,

"I'm so tired and worn I could weep.

It's my husband's demand

For a tit in each hand—

And the bastard walks 'round in his sleep!"



A cabin boy on an old clipper

Was quite a bit of a nipper;

He plugged his ass

With fragments of glass

And circumcised the skipper.

$A$ damsel, seductive and handsome,

Got wedged in a sleeping-room transom.

When she offered much gold

For release, she was told

That the view was worth more than the ransom.

In the Garden of Eden lay Adam

Complacently stroking his madam,

And loud was his mirth

For he knew that on earth

There were only two balls—and he had 'em.




There was a young fellow named Cass

Whose balls were made of spun glass.

He'd clink them together

And play *Stormy Weather*,

While lightning shot out of his ass.

There was a young lady named Hilda

Who went driving one night with a builda.

He said that he should

That he could and he would,

And he did and it pretty near killda.


Ethnologists up with the Sioux

Wired home for two punts, one canoe.

The answer next day

Said, "Girls on the way,

But what the hell's a 'panoe'?"

There was a young man from Racine

Who invented a fucking machine:

    Both concave and convex,

    It would fit either sex—

And so perfectly simple to clean!


There was a young lady named Wylde

Who kept herself quite undefiled

    By thinking of Jesus

    Contagious diseases,

And the bother of having a child.

There was a young fellow named Charteris

Put his hand where his young lady's garter is.

She said, "I don't mind,

Up higher you'll find

The place where my pisser and farter is."



There once was a young man of Kent

Whose tool was so long that it bent.

To save himself trouble

He put it in double—

And instead of coming, he went!

From the depths of the crypt at St. Giles

Came a scream that resounded for miles.

Said the vicar, "Good gracious!

Has Father Ignatius

Forgotten the Bishop has piles?"

There was a young man from St. Paul

Whose cock was exceedingly small.

    Now it might do for a keyhole

    Or a little girl's peehole

But for a big girl like me—mmmm—not at all!


I dined with the Duchess of Lee

Who asked, "Do you fart when you pee?"

    Replied I, with quick wit,

    "Do you belch when you shit?

Say, Duchess, chalk one up for me."

Cecilia of ample proportions

Took all contraceptive precautions,

But thin little Ermintrude

Let a small sperm intrude.

Do you know a good guy for abortions?

There was a young man from Brighton

Who thought he'd at last found a tight 'un.

He said, "O my love,

It fits like a glove."

Said she, "You're not in the right 'un."

There once was a monk of Camyre

Who was seized with a carnal desire.

    And the primary cause

    Was the abbess' drawers

Which were hung up to dry by the fire.

There was a young fellow of Buckingham,

Wrote a treatise on cunts and on fucking 'em;

But later this work

Was eclipsed by a Turk

Wrote an opus on ass-holes and sucking 'em.



There was a young lady named Smith

Whose virtue was largely a myth.

We knew that she did it;

She couldn't have hid it—

The question was only who with.

There was a young man of Bengal

Who swore he had only one ball,

But two sons-of-bitches

Pulled off his britches,

And the bastard had no balls at all.


There was an aesthetic young miss

Who thought it the apex of bliss

To jazz herself silly

With the bud of a lily,

Then go to the garden and piss!

The Prince of Montezuma

Once had an affair with a puma.

The puma in play

Clawed both balls away:

An example of animal humor.

There was a young fellow of Reading

Who grew quite aroused at his wedding;

   Took one look at his bride,

   Then rushed to her side,

But creamed all over the bedding.



Said a pretty young student from Smith

Whose virtue was largely a myth,

   "Try hard as I can,

   I can't find a man

Whom it's fun to be virtuous with."

There was a young man from Rangoon

Whose farts could be heard on the moon.

When you least would expect 'em,

They'd rush from his rectum,

Like the roar of a double bassoon.

There was a young lad of St. John's

Who wanted to bugger the swans,

But the loyal hall porter

Said, "No! Take my daughter.

Them birds is reserved for the dons."

An agreeable girl named Miss Doves

Likes to jack off the young men she loves.

　　She will use her bare fist

　　If the fellows insist

But she really prefers to wear gloves.

There was a young fellow from China

Whose sense of verse was much finer.

　　He thought it divine

　　To end the last line

Quite suddenly.

# Index

of last word of first line